Steve Jenkins & Robin Page

WHY DO ELEPHANTS HAVE BIG EARS

Questions—and Surprising Answers—About Animals

LB
Little, Brown and Company
New York Boston

Why do camels have a hump?

On long treks through the desert, a camel can go for days without food. It survives by living off fat stored in its hump. Many animals—bears, for example—accumulate fat in a layer all over their bodies, which helps keep them warm. In the scorching desert temperatures, however, storing fat this way could make the camel overheat. Keeping its fat in a hump allows the rest of the camel's body to cool off more easily.

Why do **bats** hang upside down?

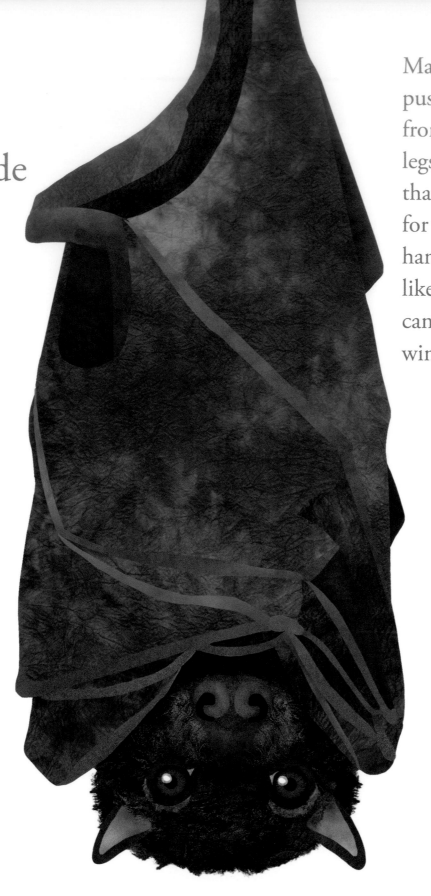

Many birds take flight by pushing off from a perch or from the ground with their legs. Some bats have legs that are too small and weak for them to do this. But by hanging upside down—like this flying fox—a bat can simply let go, open its wings, and fly away.

Why do **aye-ayes** have a long, thin middle finger?

The aye-aye has an unusual way of capturing the insects it eats. It taps on trees with its very long middle finger, listening for a hollow space where insect larvae live beneath the bark. When it hears one, the aye-aye gnaws a hole in the tree, probes the opening with the same finger, and snags its prey.

Why do
zebras
have stripes?

Scientists have a few ideas. When a herd of zebras runs to escape danger, it becomes a confusing mass of black-and-white stripes. This makes it difficult for a lion or other predator to pick out a single zebra to chase. Biting flies are also puzzled by a zebra's stripes and are less likely to land and bite. A third possibility is that the sun heats the black stripes more than the white, creating small air currents that help keep the zebra cool. Of course, it's possible that all these theories are correct.

Why do **flamingos** stand on one leg?

One theory was that the bird, which is often standing in water that is cooler than the air, did this to conserve its body heat. But scientists now believe that flamingos stand on one leg because it's easier. When balanced with its weight resting on a single leg, the flamingo can lock the joints in its standing leg so that almost no energy is expended.

Why do
spotted skunks
do handstands?

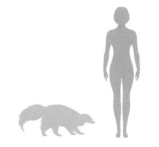

The skunk defends itself with a stinky liquid it squirts from glands under its tail. Before it sprays, the spotted skunk sends a warning by stomping its feet, standing on its front legs, and arching its tail over its back. This makes the skunk look more threatening. Often this handstand is the last warning before spraying its target.

Why do
hippos
swish their tail
when they poop?

The hippopotamus is territorial—it will claim part of a river, lake, or shoreline as its own. The hippo marks its territory by rapidly swishing its tail as it poops, scattering dung in all directions. This warns other males to stay away from the area.

Why do giraffes have a long neck?

The giraffe's long neck and legs allow it to feed on leaves and stems that shorter grazing animals can't reach. Giraffes also use their long necks in mating battles. Males batter each other with their head and neck, and the giraffe with the longest, strongest neck tends to win these fights. The giraffe's height can also allow it to spot predators from a long way off.

Why are sloths so slow?

Sloths live in the rain forest, where there are many predators. Moving slowly through the treetops helps the sloth stay hidden from eagles, jaguars, and other hunters. But the sloth couldn't move quickly even if it wanted to. Its diet is mostly hard-to-digest leaves, which don't provide enough energy for rapid movement.

Why are naked mole rats naked?

These little rodents inhabit underground burrows in the hot climate of eastern Africa. Fur is rarely needed here for warmth, and animals that live in the dark don't need a coat to protect their skin from the sun. Plus, fur can be a breeding ground for dangerous parasites.

Why do
giant squid
have huge eyes?

The giant squid has eyes the size of a dinner plate—the largest of any animal. But these creatures live deep in the sea, where no light penetrates. What use are eyes in such darkness? The giant squid's main predator is the sperm whale. As a whale moves through the water, it disturbs tiny bioluminescent animals, or light-producing animals, which begin to glow. The squid can see these faint lights warning it to escape.

Why do
chameleons
have a
long tongue?

With a body that can change color to blend into its surroundings, the chameleon sneaks up on the insects it hunts. Its feet are perfect for grasping tree branches, but they don't allow for quick lunges. So when it gets close enough, this lizard snatches up its prey by shooting out a sticky tongue that can be longer than its body.

Why do male proboscis monkeys have a big nose?

A big nose shows female monkeys that a male is strong and healthy and will make a good mate. The proboscis, or nose, also makes the male's call louder and deeper, which appeals to females.

Why do **red-eyed tree frogs** have big red eyes?

This tiny frog sleeps during the day, and its big eyes help it see at night. They also help in another way. If a hungry bird or snake wakes the frog during the day, it pops open its eyes. The sudden appearance of two bright red orbs can startle the predator, giving the tree frog a chance to escape.

Why are polar bears white?

A polar bear's fur coat isn't white. Instead, its hairs are transparent. The bear looks white because of the way its fur scatters light. A white coat camouflages the bear as it stalks seals and other prey on the snow and ice of the Arctic. There's another advantage to the polar bear's fur. Its transparent hairs allow sunlight to reach the bear's black skin, helping to keep it warm.

Why do
wombats
have cube-shaped poop?

This puzzled scientists for a long time. But now we know that wombats, like many mammals, mark their territory with their droppings. They leave their poop on top of rocks or logs, where it is easily noticed by other wombats. The shape of the droppings prevents them from rolling off.

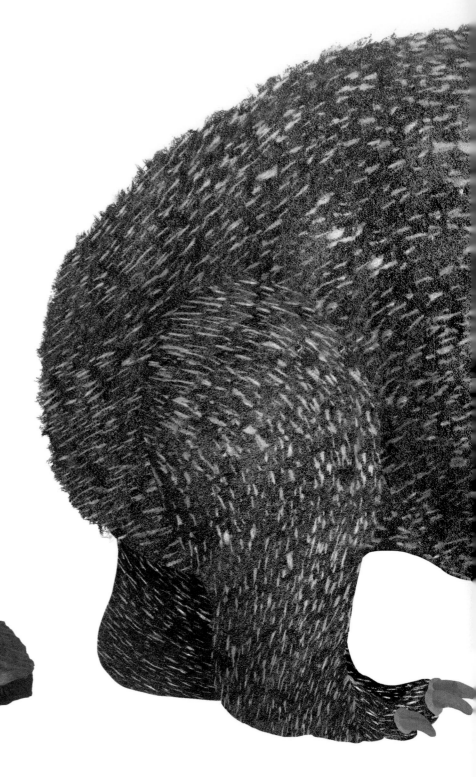

Why do hatchetfish have lights on their belly?

The hatchetfish lives deep in the sea, where only a faint glimmer of light comes from above. Predators often lurk below, watching for the shape of their prey silhouetted against the surface. The hatchetfish can produce its own light. It makes itself disappear by adjusting the brightness of the glowing spots on its belly to match the light coming from above.

Why do **narwhals** have a tusk?

The narwhal's tusk is an oversize front tooth that has grown right through the whale's lip. It is mostly found on males, but some females also grow tusks. The male narwhals with the longest tusks are favored by females looking for a mate. The narwhal's porous tusk may also sense chemicals released in the water by a potential mate, as well as other changes like temperature and salt levels. Narwhals have been observed using their tusk to whack and stun the fish they hunt.

Why do African elephants have big ears?

African elephants live in a hot climate, and they need a way to cool off. Their huge ears act like radiators, shedding excess heat. By fanning them back and forth, the elephant cools itself even more. And big ears are useful in other ways. When danger threatens, elephants spread their ears to make themselves look larger and more intimidating. Finally, big ears can help focus sound and enhance the elephant's hearing.

A camel with one hump is called a dromedary or **Arabian camel**. Bactrian camels have two humps. Both have been domesticated for thousands of years. Arabian camels are found in the Middle East, North Africa, central and southern Asia, and Australia. They live in dry or desert habitats and eat grasses and shrubs. A camel can weigh as much as 1,500 pounds (680 kilograms), and it can go several weeks without drinking water. The camel, with a top speed of about 25 miles per hour (40 kilometers per hour), is not as fast as a horse, but it can outrun a horse on the sands of the desert.

 The **large flying fox** is a kind of fruit bat. It's one of the biggest bats in the world, with a wingspan of up to 5 feet (1½ meters). These bats live in the tropical forests and orchards of Southeast Asia and the islands of the southwest Pacific and Indian Oceans. They eat fruit, flowers, and nectar. Though the large flying fox is active at night, it doesn't echolocate—navigate by sound—the way most bats do. Instead it relies on its large eyes and keen sense of smell.

 The **aye-aye** is found only on the island of Madagascar. It lives in the rain forest and spends almost its entire life in the treetops. Aye-ayes are a kind of lemur, with a body about 15 inches (38 centimeters) long, not including the tail. They sleep during the day and forage for insects, fruit, seeds, and other plant foods at night. Aye-ayes are endangered. The forests where they live are being cut down or burned to make room for farms and houses.

 The zebra in this book is a **plains zebra**. It lives in the grasslands and forests of eastern and southern Africa. A zebra can be 8 feet (2½ meters) long and weigh as much as 850 pounds (386 kilograms). It has black skin with a unique pattern of black-and-white stripes. Zebras live in family groups that often gather to form large herds. A zebra can run at speeds up to 43 miles per hour (70 kilometers per hour). If it can't outrun a lion or hyena, the zebra tries to defend itself with bites and a powerful kick.

 Averaging 4½ feet (137 centimeters) in height, the **greater flamingo** is the largest species of flamingo. These flamingos are found in southern Europe, western and southern Asia, and parts of Africa. They gather in large flocks—sometimes called a flamboyance—in saltwater marshes, lakes, and along coastlines. Wading through shallow water, a flamingo uses its beak to filter out shrimp and other small creatures as well as algae and plant matter. The birds' brilliant pink color comes from the food they eat. Flamingos in a zoo that don't digest these pigments will turn white.

 The **spotted skunk** is common throughout southern Canada, the United States, and northern Mexico. A skunk can shoot its stinky liquid, called musk, up to 15 feet (4½ meters). It can temporarily blind an attacker. Foxes, coyotes, and most other predators usually avoid skunks, especially if they've ever been sprayed. Owls, hawks, and other birds of prey are the biggest threat to a skunk because they attack from above and are not easily targeted by the skunk's spray. The striped skunk's body is about 2 feet (61 centimeters) long. It inhabits a wide range of habitats, including forests, fields, and human settlements. Skunks are omnivores—they eat insects, rodents, frogs, small reptiles, bird's eggs, plant foods, and garbage.

 The **hippopotamus** can reach 14 feet (4¼ meters) in length and weigh as much as 8,000 pounds (3,629 kilograms). It's the third largest living land animal—only the elephant and the white rhinoceros are bigger. Hippos live near rivers, lakes, and swamps throughout central and southern Africa. They spend most of the day submerged in water, coming out at night to graze on grass and other plants. When they do spend time in the sun, they secrete a red oily substance that is a natural sunscreen and that led to the myth that hippos sweat blood. Despite its bulky body, a hippopotamus can run faster than a human. Male hippos fiercely defend their territory. This makes them one of the most dangerous animals in the world, killing an estimated five hundred people every year.

 Reaching 19 feet in height (almost 6 meters), the **giraffe** is the tallest living land animal. Giraffes roam the plains and woodlands of central and southern Africa. They feed on leaves, stems, grass, and fruit using their long tongue, which can reach 18 inches (46 centimeters), to pluck hard-to-reach foliage. Lions, leopards, and other large predators prey on giraffes, especially young or sick animals. A healthy adult giraffe is not an easy meal. It can run as fast as 35 miles per hour (56 kilometers per hour) and, if cornered, defend itself with a kick that can kill a lion.

 The **pale-throated three-toed sloth** is about 2 feet (61 centimeters) long and weighs about as much as a cat. It spends almost all its life hanging upside down in the treetops. It is the world's slowest mammal, but it's a surprisingly good swimmer, sometimes dropping from a branch into the water to escape danger. Sloths have powerful curved claws that can grip a branch and hold on even when they are asleep. And they sleep a lot—as much as twenty hours a day. Algae grows on the sloth's fur, which gives it a green tint and helps it hide from predators. Sloths eat leaves that would be poisonous to most animals. An unusual digestive system breaks down these leaves, but it is a slow and inefficient process that doesn't provide much energy. A sloth only climbs down from its tree to poop. This is when it's in the most danger from jaguars, snakes, and other predators. If it's attacked, the sloth will defend itself with its teeth and claws.

 Naked mole rats spend their entire lives underground. They create a maze of burrows and tunnels under arid grasslands, where they feed on plant roots, bulbs, and tubers. About 3 to 4 inches (7 to 10 centimeters) long, these unusual little rodents live in colonies of typically forty to eighty extended family members. The colonies are similar to an ant nest or beehive. Soldiers guard the colony, workers dig and repair tunnels, and a queen produces all the babies. Unlike most mammals, naked mole rats' body temperature changes with the environment, so they must huddle together for warmth or find cooler chambers in the heat. They don't drink water, getting all they need from their food. And they can live thirty years or more—longer than any other rodent.

 Although **giant squid** inhabit all the world's oceans, scientists had never seen one alive until 2004, when one was photographed with a remote deep-sea camera. These enormous creatures can reach around 43 feet (13 meters) in length. Their eyes can be 10½ inches (27 centimeters) in diameter. Like all squid, they have eight arms and two long tentacles. These tentacles are tipped with sharp-edged suction cups and are used to capture fish and other squid. Giant squid spend most of their time deep in the ocean but occasionally chase their prey into shallower waters.

 The **veiled chameleon** is a tree-dwelling reptile that lives in the Middle Eastern countries of Yemen and Saudi Arabia. Males are large, growing to 2 feet (61 centimeters) in length. Females are about half that size. These lizards eat insects and some plants, which they rely on as a source of water. Chameleons are famous for their ability to change color. The veiled chameleon's natural coloration is a mottled green with blue, brown, and yellow markings. This camouflages the chameleon in its treetop habitat. It changes color to communicate with other chameleons or to show that it is frightened or angry. If it is excited or aggressive, its colors brighten. A fearful or sick chameleon will become dull brown. And a cold one will turn dark to help it absorb sunlight and warm up.

 The **proboscis monkey** lives only on the island of Borneo in the southwest Pacific Ocean. Males are larger than females, reaching 28 inches (71 centimeters) in length. These monkeys live near rivers, coastlines, and swamps. They spend most of their time in the trees, but they are excellent swimmers and often leap from a tree into the water. Their diet consists of seeds, leaves, fruit, and insects.

 During the day, the **red-eyed tree frog** sleeps with its eyes closed and its colorful legs tucked beneath it. The membranes that cover its eyes are green but slightly transparent. This allows it to see danger approaching. The frog startles a predator by suddenly changing from what looks like a green clump of leaves into a creature with big red eyes and bright blue legs. At 3 inches (7½ centimeters) in length, female red-eyed tree frogs are a little bigger than males. These frogs rarely leave the trees, where they hunt and eat insects—and sometimes other frogs. They inhabit the forests of southern Mexico, Central America, and northern South America.

 A male **polar bear** can weigh more than 1,500 pounds (680 kilograms). It is the largest living predator on land, and it prowls the coastlines and sea ice of the Arctic as it hunts seals, beluga whales, and other prey. It often practices still-hunting, lying quietly near a seal's breathing hole in the ice. When the seal surfaces to take a breath, the bear seizes it. It also preys on seal pups, digging them out of their dens in the snow. Polar bears usually avoid humans, but they can be unpredictable and dangerous, and have sometimes killed and eaten people. It wouldn't be easy to escape a charging bear—it can run as fast as a horse over a short distance.

 The **common wombat** lives in the forests and open shrublands of southeastern Australia and the island of Tasmania. This marsupial mammal, a relative of the koala and kangaroo, is about 40 inches (1 meter) long. It is a herbivore that feeds on grass, shrubs, roots, and bark. Wombats sleep in burrows in the daytime and forage at dusk and during the night. Their cube-shaped droppings are formed by the unusual structure of their intestines. The wombat can be a formidable foe for a predator. The back of its body is reinforced with cartilage. If it is threatened, the wombat gets into its burrow and uses its rear end to block the entrance. If the attacker manages to get its head past this obstacle, the wombat uses its legs to crush the intruder's head against the ceiling of the burrow.

 The **giant hatchetfish** gets its name from its thin body, which looks like the blade of a hatchet. Its back half looks like a handle, adding to the effect. Though it is the largest species of hatchetfish, it is less than 5 inches (12 centimeters) long. Giant hatchetfish are common throughout the world's oceans, except for the polar regions. Their diet includes animal plankton—tiny creatures that drift through the water—and small shellfish. Hatchetfish hunt by looking up and watching for prey that is silhouetted by the dim light coming from the surface.

Narwhals spend their lives in the cold Arctic waters around Canada, Greenland, and Russia. Like all whales, they are warm-blooded and breathe air. A big narwhal can be 18 feet (5½ meters) long, not including its tusk, which can reach 10 feet (3 meters) in length. It preys on fish, shrimp, and squid. Hundreds of years ago, traders brought narwhal tusks from the Arctic to Europe and sold them as unicorn horns. Europeans believed the horns had magical properties.

 There are two species of **African elephant**. The bush elephant, the one in this book, is larger than its relative, the forest elephant. Both are larger than any other animal living on land. A big male bush elephant can weigh up to 14,000 pounds (6,300 kilograms) and stand 13 feet (4 meters) tall at the shoulder. Bush elephants live in family groups in the open grasslands of central and southern Africa. These groups are led by an older female and include other females, immature males, and babies. An elephant can consume 330 pounds (150 kilograms) of food a day. It uses its trunk to pluck the grass, leaves, and tree branches it eats. An elephant trunk is an amazing tool. It is used for breathing, drinking, making sounds, and grasping things. It's strong enough to uproot a tree and delicate enough to handle an egg without breaking it. The elephant's trunk contains more than forty thousand muscles, compared to around six hundred in an entire human body.

Bibliography

Attenborough, David. *The Life of Mammals.* Princeton, NJ: Princeton University Press, 2002.

Clarke, Ginjer. *The Fascinating Animal Book for Kids: 500 Wild Facts!* Emeryville, CA: Rockridge Press, 2020.

Cliffe, Rebecca. *Sloths: Life in the Slow Lane.* Preston, UK: Sloth Conservation Foundation, 2017.

Flannery, Tim. *Weird, Wild, Amazing! Exploring the Incredible World of Animals.* New York: Norton Young Readers, 2020.

Hare, Tony. *Animal Fact File: Head-to-Tail Profiles of More Than 90 Mammals.* New York: Checkmark Books, 1999.

Hoare, Ben. *An Anthology of Intriguing Animals.* New York: DK Children, 2018.

Holmes, Martha, and Michael Gunton. *Life: Extraordinary Animals, Extreme Behaviour.* Berkeley: University of California Press, 2010.

Hoyt, Erich. *Creatures of the Deep: In Search of the Sea's "Monsters" and the World They Live In.* Buffalo, NY: Firefly Books, 2001.

Lovett, Sarah. *Extremely Weird Primates.* Santa Fe, NM: John Muir Publications, 1991.

Wood, Amanda, and Mike Jolley. *Natural World.* New York: Wide Eyed Editions, 2016.

For Ash Stephen Scott. In memory of Steve.

About This Book: The illustrations for this book were done in collage and Adobe Photoshop. This book was edited by Margaret Raymo and designed by Brenda E. Angelilli with art direction by Saho Fujii. The production was supervised by Kimberly Stella, and the production editor was Marisa Finkelstein. The text was set in Adobe Garamond Pro and Proxima Nova, and the display type is Adobe Garamond Pro.

Little, Brown and Company
Hachette Book Group
1290 Avenue of the Americas, New York, NY 10104
Visit us at LBYR.com

First Edition: November 2023

Little, Brown and Company is a division of Hachette Book Group, Inc.

The Little, Brown name and logo are trademarks of Hachette Book Group, Inc.

The publisher is not responsible for websites (or their content) that are not owned by the publisher.

Little, Brown and Company books may be purchased in bulk for business, educational, or promotional use. For information, please contact your local bookseller or the Hachette Book Group Special Markets Department at special.markets@hbgusa.com.

Library of Congress Cataloging-in-Publication Data
Names: Jenkins, Steve, 1952–2021, author. | Page, Robin, author.
Title: Why do elephants have big ears? : questions—and surprising answers—about animals / by Steve Jenkins, and Robin Page.
Other titles: Questions—and surprising answers—about animals / Description: First edition. | New York : Little, Brown and Company, 2023. | Includes bibliographical references. | Audience: Ages 4–8 | Summary: "Strange, exciting, and interesting facts explore the wonderful world of animals." —Provided by publisher.
Identifiers: LCCN 2022045871 | ISBN 9780316456791 (hardcover)
Subjects: LCSH: Animals—Juvenile literature. | Animals—Miscellanea—Juvenile literature.
Classification: LCC QL49 .J579 2023 | DDC 590—dc23/eng/20220929
LC record available at https://lccn.loc.gov/2022045871

ISBN 978-0-316-45679-1

PRINTED IN CHINA

APS

10 9 8 7 6 5 4 3 2 1